Caterpillar

A Healing Journal

WITH BIBLE REFERENCES

Tiffanie Sibert

ISBN: 979-8-218-39370-0

This journal belongs to You!
Follow the flow, skip around, take a break if things get too heavy. Do what feels natural for you.
This is a safe space for you to be with yourself, so there are no expectations; no right nor wrong.
Healing and love.

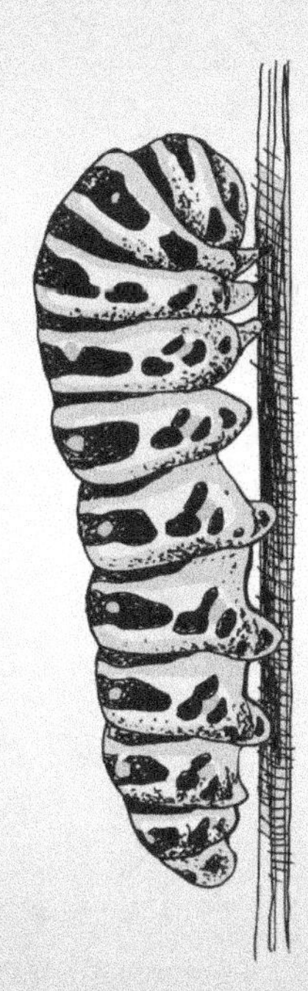

_____ / _____ / _____

Today, I am grateful for:

Journal

The Lord is my light and my salvation; whom shall I fear? the Lord is the
strength of my life; of whom shall I be afraid? - Psalm 27:1 (KJV)

Today, I am grateful for:

<u>Journal</u>

Yea, I have loved thee with an everlasting love: therefore with lovingkindness have I drawn thee. - Jeremiah 31:3 (KJV)

____ / ____ / ____

Today, I am grateful for:

Journal

Neither shall they say, Lo here! or, lo there! for, behold, the kingdom of God is within you.
– Luke 17:21 (KJV)

_____ / _____ / _____

Today, I am grateful for:

____

<u>Journal</u>

Then shall the righteous shine forth as the sun in the kingdom of their
Father. Who hath ears to hear, let him hear. – Matthew 13:43 (KJV)

Today, I am grateful for:

____

Journal

For it became him, for whom are all things, and by whom are all things, in bringing many sons unto glory, to make the captain of their salvation perfect through sufferings. – Hebrews 2:10 (KJV)

_____ / _____ / _____

Today, I am grateful for:

____

<u>Journal</u>

____

____

____

____

____

____

____

____

____

____

____

____

____

____

____

____

But the meek shall inherit the earth; and shall delight themselves in the abundance of peace.
– Psalm 37:11 (KJV)

_____/_____/_____

Today, I am grateful for:

____

<u>Journal</u>

And the Lord shall help them, and deliver them: he shall deliver them from the wicked, and save them, because they trust in him. - Psalm 37:40 (KJV)

Today, I am grateful for:

<u>Journal</u>

Hear my voice, O God, in my prayer: preserve my life from fear of the enemy.
– Psalm 64:1 (KJV)

Today, I am grateful for:

Journal

The righteous shall be glad in the Lord, and shall trust in him; and
all the upright in heart shall glory. – Psalm 64:10 (KJV)

Today, I am grateful for:

____

<u>Journal</u>

Today, I am grateful for:

____

<u>Journal</u>

No weapon that is formed against thee shall prosper; and every tongue that shall rise against thee in judgment thou shalt condemn. – Isaiah 54:17 (KJV)

Today, I am grateful for:

<u>Journal</u>

In the fear of the Lord is strong confidence: and his children shall have a place of refuge.
– Proverbs 14:26 (KJV)

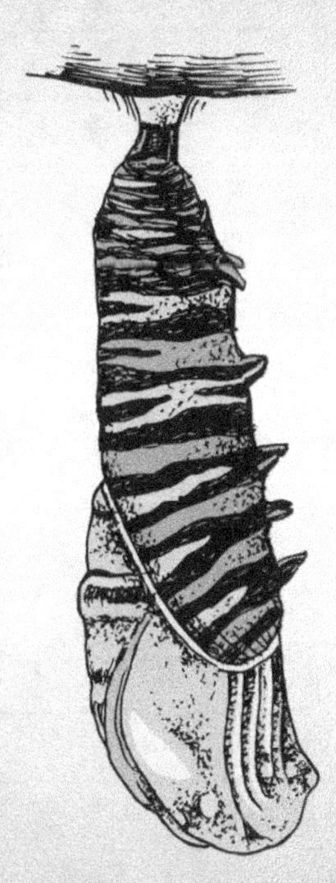

Today, I will:

____

<u>Journal</u>

Protect your heart.

Today, I will:

____

Journal

____
____
____
____
____
____
____
____
____
____
____
____
____
____
____

Show love to yourself.

_____/_____/_____

Today, I will:

____

<u>*Journal*</u>

Rest.

_____ / _____ / _____

Today, I will:

____

Journal

____
____
____
____
____
____
____
____
____
____
____
____
____
____

Give yourself grace.

_____ / _____ /_____

Today, I will:

____

<u>Journal</u>

Embrace the sunshine.

Today, I will:

Journal

Be still.

_____ / _____ / _____

Today, I will:

<u>Journal</u>

Breathe good in; breathe out the bad.

_____ / _____ / _____

Today, I will:

____

<u>Journal</u>

Pray every day.

Today, I will:

_____ / _____ / _____

____

<u>Journal</u>

Self-soothe.

Today, I will:

<u>*Journal*</u>

Meditate.

_____ / _____ / _____

Today, I will:

<u>Journal</u>

Ground yourself in the earth.

_____ / _____ / _____

Today, I will:

<u>*Journal*</u>

Healing is not a race.

_____ / _____ / _____

Today, I will:

____

<u>Journal</u>

Move your body.

Today, I will:

Journal

Nourish and replenish.

_____ / _____ /

Today, I will:

<u>Journal</u>

Hug yourself and others.

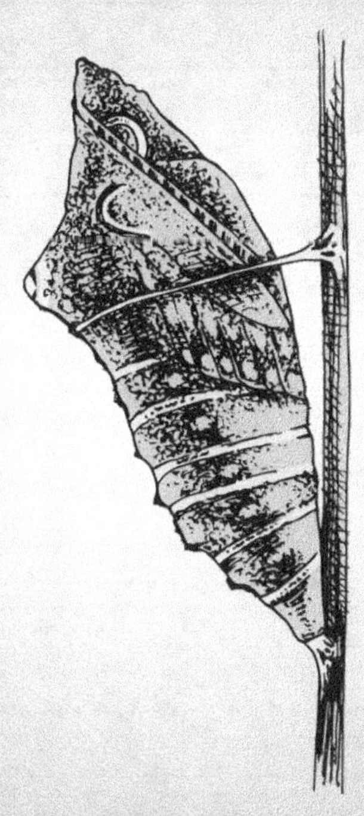

I trust God with:

____

____

____

____

____

____

____

____

____

____

____

____

____

____

____

____

_____ / _____ / _____

Love is:

You are approved by God.

_____ / _____ /

Love is not:

Trust your intuition.

I was hurt when:

_____/_____/_____

I forgive myself for:

I forgive others for:

____

____

____

____

____

____

____

____

____

____

____

____

____

____

____

____

*"For if ye forgive men their trespasses, your heavenly Father
will also forgive you..." – Matthew 6:14 (KJV)*

_____/_____/_____

I am free when:

I am joyful when:

Real support looks like:

_____ / _____

I will prioritize:

Fill your cup first.

_____ / _____ / _____

Self-love means and looks like:

God loves you.

I am walking away from:

____

____

____

____

____

____

____

____

____

____

____

____

____

____

____

I dream of:

Explore!

My goals are:

Dream it. Believe it. Achieve it.

I value:

You are worthy!

_____ / _____ / _____

I trust that:

You deserve God's best.

I am planning to:

____

____

____

____

____

____

____

____

____

____

____

____

____

____

____

____

____

____

____

Stay focused.

I am healing from:

_____ / _____ /

I am letting go of:

Release what does not serve you.

I rest when:

Be still.

I give myself grace when:

____

____

____

____

____

____

____

____

____

____

____

____

____

____

____

____

Have faith.

I give myself credit for:

____

____

____

____

____

____

____

____

____

____

____

____

____

____

____

____

____

_____/_____/_____

I am worthy of:

You are priceless.

_____ / ___ / _____

I love others because:

You are a child of God.

I am intentional about:

Practice mindfulness.

_____ / _____ / _____

I am enough, even on days when:

You are more than enough!

What are my boundaries?

How do I regulate (manage) my emotions?

How do I self-soothe?

How does nature contribute to my healing?

What are my insecurities and how can I face them?

_____ / _____ / _____

How does my heart feel?

_____ / _____ / _____

In what ways can I protect my power and peace?

How do I honor myself and others?

In what ways do I show myself love?

_____ / _____ / _____

What is or what do I believe is my purpose? And why?

How can I cope with and overcome my insecurities?

What fears and resentments am I holding onto?

_____ / _____ / _____

What lessons has heartbreak taught me?

When life is uncomfortable or when faced with a challenge, how do I react or respond? How can I better manage my emotions during uncertain times?

What am I grieving?

_____ / _____ /_____

What do I need to feel safe?

How can I carve out time for myself each day?

I will set boundaries by:

(List your responses in the bullet points.)

-
-
-
-
-
-

I will make better choices and decisions by:

(List your responses in the bullet points.)

-

-

-

-

-

-

_____/_____/_____

I will practice self-discipline by:

(List your responses in the bullet points.)

-
-
-
-
-
-

_____/_____/_____

I will stay close to God by:

(List your responses in the bullet points.)

-
-
-
-
-
-

_____/_____/_____

I will choose and attract healthier relationships by:

(List your responses in the bullet points.)

-

-

-

-

-

-

_____/_____/_____

I will show up better in the world by:

(List your responses in the bullet points.)

-
-
-
-
-
-

_____/_____/_____

I will release control by:

(List your responses in the bullet points.)

-

-

-

-

-

-

_____ / _____ / _____

I will release what does not belong to me by:

(List your responses in the bullet points.)

-

-

-

-

-

-

_____/_____/_____

My top 5 values are:

(List your responses in the bullet points.)

-

-

-

-

-

What wounds are attached to my current patterns and decisions?

(List your responses in the bullet points.)

-

-

-

-

-

-

What do I have a hard time letting go of?

(*List your responses in the bullet points.*)

-

-

-

-

-

-

_____ / _____ / _____

<u>*Letter to Yourself*</u>

Dear CHILD _____________________ *(Your Name),*

____

____

____

____

____

____

____

____

____

____

____

____

____

____

____

____

____

Love always,

<u>Letter to Yourself</u>

Dear CHILD _____________________ (Your Name),

____

____

____

____

____

____

____

____

____

____

____

____

____

____

____

____

Love always,

<u>Letter to Yourself</u>

Dear CHILD __________________ (Your Name),

Love always,

_____ / _____ / _____

<u>Letter to Yourself</u>

Dear CHILD _____________________ (Your Name),

Love always,

______/______/______

<u>Letter to Yourself</u>

Dear CHILD _____________________ (Your Name),

____

____

____

____

____

____

____

____

____

____

____

____

____

____

____

Love always,

_____/_____/_____

<u>Letter to Yourself</u>

Dear TEENAGE ___________________ (Your Name),

Love always,

_____ / ____ / _____

<u>*Letter to Yourself*</u>

Dear TEENAGE _______________________ *(Your Name),*

____

____

____

____

____

____

____

____

____

____

____

____

____

Love always,

<u>Letter to Yourself</u>

Dear TEENAGE ___________________ (Your Name),

Love always,

<u>Letter to Yourself</u>

Dear TEENAGE _______________ (Your Name),

Love always,

_____ / _____ / _____

<u>Letter to Yourself</u>

Dear TEENAGE _____________________ (Your Name),

____

____

____

____

____

____

____

____

____

____

____

____

____

____

____

____

Love always,

<u>*Letter to Yourself*</u>

Dear ADULT _____________________ *(Your Name),*

____

____

____

____

____

____

____

____

____

____

____

____

____

____

____

____

Love always,

______ / ______ / ______

<u>Letter to Yourself</u>

Dear ADULT _____________________ (Your Name),

____

____

____

____

____

____

____

____

____

____

____

____

____

____

Love always,

<u>*Letter to Yourself*</u>

Dear ADULT _____________________ *(Your Name),*

____

____

____

____

____

____

____

____

____

____

____

____

____

____

Love always,

<u>Letter to Yourself</u>

Dear ADULT __________________ (Your Name),

Love always,

_____ / _____ / _____

<u>Letter to Yourself</u>

Dear ADULT __________________ (Your Name),

____

____

____

____

____

____

____

____

____

____

____

____

____

____

Love always,

As I heal, I am growing and shifting towards:

Notes

<u>*Notes*</u>

Notes

<u>*Notes*</u>

<u>*Notes*</u>

<u>*Notes*</u>

<u>*Notes*</u>

<u>*Notes*</u>

<u>*Notes*</u>

<u>*Notes*</u>